BUILT DIFFERENT

EMBRACING IDENTITY, AUTHENTICITY, AND SELF-DISCOVERY

STUDENTS OF NORTHAMPTON COUNTY PUBLIC SCHOOLS

Copyright © 2025 by Final Step Publishing

For permissions, inquiries, or bulk orders, please contact:

Final Step Publishing
Suffolk, Virginia
Email: finalsteppub@gmail.com

BOOK TITLE:

BUILT DIFFERENT: EMBRACING IDENTITY, AUTHENTICITY, AND SELF-DISCOVERY

First Edition, 2025
ISBN: 979-8-9915622-2-5

This book is a collaborative anthology featuring original writings and artwork by students from:
Northampton High School, Northampton Early College, Conway Middle School, and Gaston STEM Leadership Academy, in partnership with the Ladies of Distinction and Max Potential Boys Mentorship programs.

Cover design and interior layout by Tessy Ogidi.
Printed in the United States of America.

DEDICATION

*This **anthology is dedicated** to the superintendents, educators, site coordinators, and parents who gave selflessly of themselves so that their students could achieve great heights, walk in purpose, and maximize their potential.*

CONTENT

LEVELING UP 03

04 MAX POTENTIAL SHORT STORIES

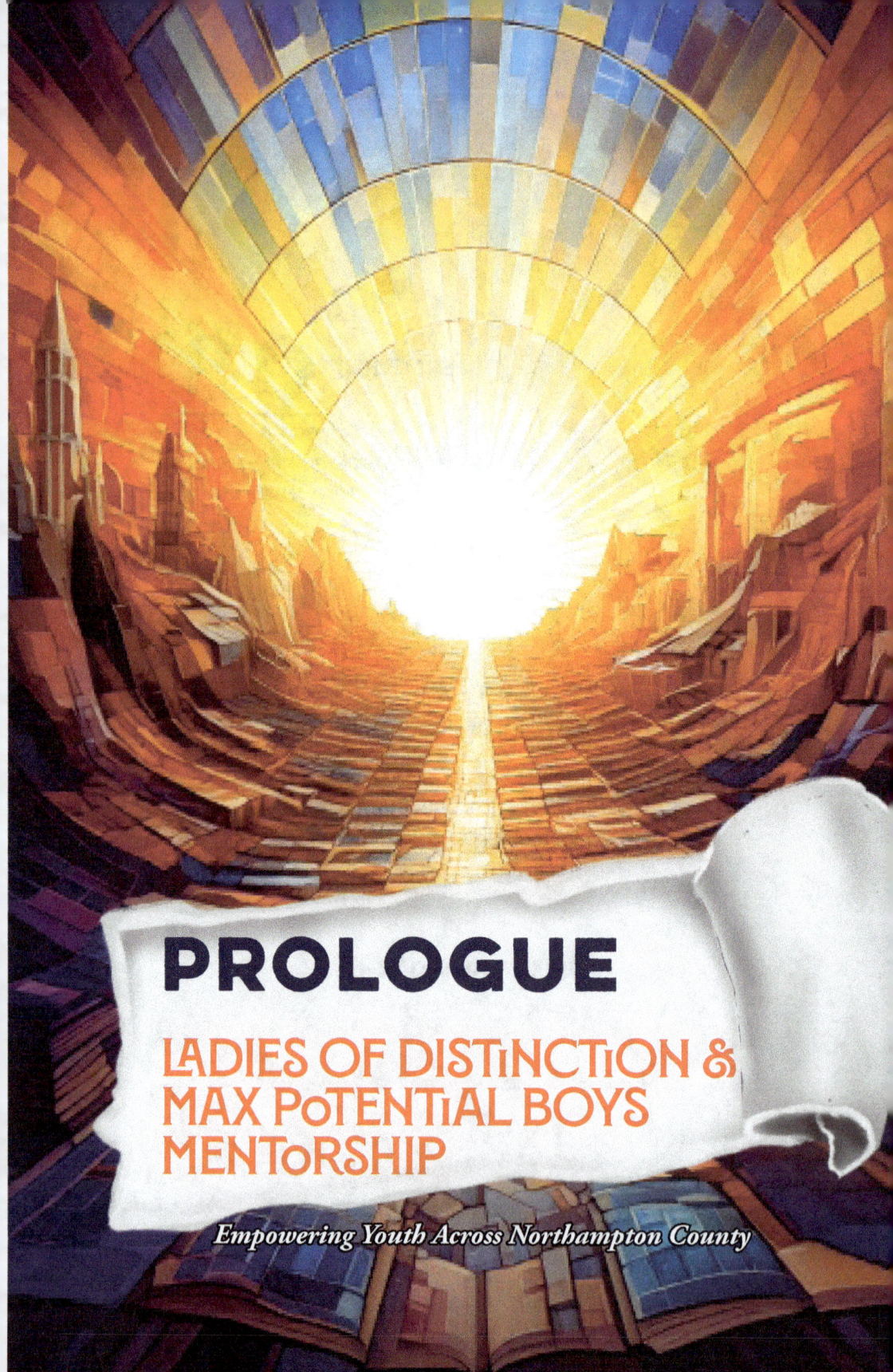

PROLOGUE

LADIES OF DISTINCTION & MAX POTENTIAL BOYS MENTORSHIP

Empowering Youth Across Northampton County

Ladies of Distinction is a young girls' empowerment program serving elementary, middle, and high school students. Founded by **Dr. Jennell Riddick**, the program is designed to foster character development, promote health and wellness, and cultivate a sense of sisterhood and leadership among girls of all ages. Participants meet weekly and gather quarterly for special events across multiple states—offering them opportunities to engage with a variety of cultures, a diversity of skills, and educational levels.

In partnership with this initiative, **Max Potential Boys Mentorship**, led by **Dr. Dwight Riddick**, provides a similar transformative experience for young men. This program helps boys connect with their identity and purpose through practical life skills, speaking exercises, business-building tips, soft skill development, relationship-building, and exposure through field trips.

Recognizing the need for deeper literacy engagement beyond traditional classroom instruction, the team launched the **School Literacy Project**—a powerful platform for students to express their voices through writing and visual art. After multiple mentorship and coaching sessions, students reflected on what they learned, how they felt, the challenges they overcame, and their overall experiences in *Ladies of Distinction and Max Potential Boys Mentorship*. While some opted to keep their reflections private, many chose to contribute their work to this collective anthology.

These programs were implemented across schools in Northampton County, North Carolina—including **Northampton High School, Northampton Early College, Conway Middle School,** and **Gaston STEM Leadership Academy.**

CHAPTER 1

FINDING MY VOICE

BECOMING A LADY OF DISTINCTION – C. JOYNER

Being in L.O.D. (Ladies of Distinction), I have learned that it's okay to be yourself—because at the end of the day, you should only be worried about yourself and nobody else. You should never think you can't say no in a situation, because you can. You have your own rights, and you should never be afraid to speak up when something is wrong. I have also learned that if you're feeling peer-pressured or feel like a certain friend group is bringing you down, separate yourself from that group and find better friends—or just be by yourself and focus on YOU and what YOU want to do. NEVER lower your standards for ANYBODY, because they could use that to take advantage of you or make you do something you know is wrong, and you end up getting in trouble while they don't. Being a lady/girl doesn't mean you should lower anything for ANY man/boy, because you are your own person, and you can only control yourself—nobody else.

Additionally, a lady of distinction embodies resilience and perseverance. Many times, women like these have faced significant challenges— whether personal, societal, or institutional—and yet they have overcome these obstacles with grace and determination. It's their ability to rise above

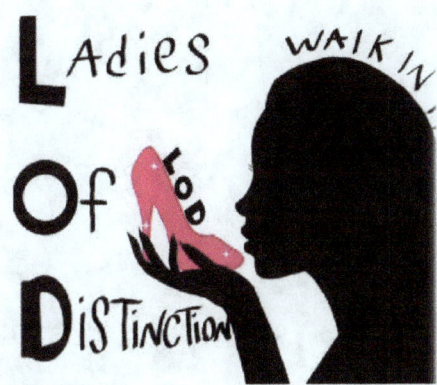

adversity that inspires me and encourages others, especially younger generations, to push past their own limitations. We see this in women who fight for equality, education, and justice, showing that perseverance is often the key to making meaningful change. Lastly, the influence of a lady of distinction goes far beyond her own achievements. It's about the way she uplifts and empowers others. Through mentorship, advocacy, and activism, women of distinction create change that affects entire communities and generations. In my own life, I strive to be a positive influence, knowing that even small actions can ripple out and make a difference.

In conclusion, I believe that being a lady of distinction isn't just about talent or status; it's about having a profound impact on others through resilience, integrity, and a relentless pursuit of excellence. It's a journey of growth and a lifelong commitment to inspiring change in the world around me.

IT IS OKAY To BE YOURSELF – D. LONG

Fitting in—whether it's in a group of friends or something in general—isn't always a good thing. At some point in your life, you are going to have to figure out that not everything is for you. Not everyone has the same mindset as you, and it's okay if absolutely no one has the same mindset as you. If you continue to hang around people you know are no good for you, your mindset could then be shifted negatively.

For example, you could hang with gossipers you want to be nothing like, but as time goes on, you shift to become a gossiper as well.

Spending more time with negative influences can lead you farther away from a community that wants to support you. You weren't put on Earth to be a people-pleaser, instead you were created to live a life that shows and reflects God's purpose and love. So yes, it's more than okay to be different.

To be yourself, you are going to have to learn yourself. Learning yourself consists of being true to yourself, along with striving to be humble and reflect love towards others without being full of pride. Remember that staying humble is very beautiful. When you do good, don't just do it expecting some kind of praise out of it—do good things simply because they are good. You will also need to have self-acceptance. Self-acceptance allows you to see the importance of knowing both your strengths and weaknesses. Isolation is not a bad thing.

Sometimes you will be put in a season of isolation, so you are able to seek connection with yourself. Remember to always know your worth and embrace your individuality. Diversity is very important. With diversity, we are able to show and be comfortable in our differences, creating strong communities.

Overall, being yourself brings a sense of peace, self-acceptance, and it encourages personal growth. It is perfectly okay to embrace your differences—for they are all unique.

LEARNING To BE ME – M. WARR!CK

Because of L.O.D., I have now realized that I need to worry about myself before I worry about others. I mean this in a good way… meaning that I need to take care of myself before I worry about others. This includes not changing myself for others, because I have realized that if I have to change myself to "fit in," then the people you change yourself for are not your real friends. Now when I say you shouldn't change yourself, I mean you should not have to change your hobbies and things you love. This could affect your mental and physical health, so NEVER change yourself about it. Another thing I have learned is to NEVER give your heart away too fast. Make people earn your trust—make them work for your love and heart. Because if you give your heart away to the wrong people too fast, it will hurt very badly.

Next thing… peer pressure. If you ever get around the wrong group of people… they may make you do the wrong things. THOSE PEOPLE ARE NOT YOUR FRIENDS! If you ever feel like you have to choose and make the wrong decisions, they are not the right people to hang around. You should also ALWAYS accept everyone, even if you don't like the same things they do or the people they hang around. You should always love yourself no matter what. Never let anyone bring you down. Let your mistakes be a lesson, not an embarrassment. Everything happens for a reason, so if you make a mistake—learn from it. Loyalty is important, so if you want loyalty, then you need to give loyalty first. If you ever see anyone doing the wrong thing, SPEAK UP!!! Don't let them do it. This leads me to my last thing. You should also always be a good friend. You should never be fake because of other people or because of what those people did to you. There are other coping mechanisms. So thank you, L.O.D., for helping me gain confidence and know right from wrong!

CHAPTER TWO

WISDOM IN ACTION

NAVIGATING NEGATIVITY – A. HARVEY

In today's world, negativity can come from many places: social media, news outlets, personal relationships, and perhaps the most powerful of all—our own inner thoughts. Negative thinking can consume you. What makes this kind of negativity so dangerous is how real it feels. It's not the voice of a stranger or a friend—it's your own. That's what makes it hurt the most, because when your own mind tells you that you're not enough, it feels familiar and believable. When you're struggling with negativity in your mind, it's like a storm clouds your vision. Everything you do, say, or think feels useless, unintelligent, or unimportant. The scariest part is that no one else can hear the war going on inside your head. On the outside, you might look completely okay. But inside, you're carrying a heavy, invisible burden that feels almost impossible to explain.

As someone who has dealt with a lot of negativity, my biggest advice is to take a moment and recognize what you have. A lot of teenagers see gratitude as a chore—something adults make you do to be polite. But in reality, gratitude can be one of your greatest sources of encouragement. It's easy to get

caught in the rain and forget to look up, but if you take a moment, you'll notice the beautiful shapes the clouds make. Next time you feel disappointed or lost, pause and think about what you've accomplished, what you're thankful for, or even what you're looking forward to. In a world that often feels cold and unforgiving, holding on to your blessings can help you stay motivated. Gratitude won't erase the storms, but it can help you understand that rainbows are soon to come. So, when the world feels a little colder, remember, spring is coming.

ITS OKAY To SAY NO

I think the word "No" has probably been one of the hardest things I've had to learn how to start saying. It's so easy for people to want to be overly nice in such a cruel world, but I'm here to tell you—you have to say no. Because if you don't, no one will respect you.

My history with learning how to say "no" was hard. I used to struggle with being a doormat, constantly letting people walk all over me just to avoid conflict or disappointing anyone. I thought that being nice meant always being available, always saying yes, always putting others first— even if it hurt me. I didn't want to seem difficult, or like I didn't care. So I agreed. I went along with things I didn't want to do.

But the truth is, no one ever took into consideration how I was feeling, until I finally said "no."

Of course, there's the obvious reason why you should feel comfortable telling people "no": because *you* matter. Besides that very important fact, if you let people know that you are willing to do anything and everything, in their eyes, your value goes down. I mean, think about it, if you eat your favorite food every single day, will it be your favorite anymore? Or will you get used to the taste? Too much of anything is bad, including saying yes to everything. When you constantly make yourself available, people start to expect it. They stop appreciating your effort because they assume you'll always be there—even at the cost of your own time, energy, or happiness. And that's not fair to you. Sometimes, the real strength isn't in giving or sacrificing—it's in protecting. Protecting your spirit. You have to protect the parts of *you* that the world will take for granted. Unless you learn to say no, you'll find yourself pouring from an empty cup, wondering why you're always so tired and feel so unseen.

My history with learning how to say no was hard. I struggled with being a doormat and letting people run over me. No one ever took into consideration how I was feeling until I said no.

IF THE SHOE DON'T FIT, DON'T WEAR IT — C. BOONE

You've probably heard the saying, "If the shoe don't fit, don't wear it." And yeah, it's not really about shoes—it's about life. Basically, it means if something isn't right for you, don't force it. Whether it's a trend, a friendship, or a certain path in life, not everything that works for someone else is meant for you. And that's okay.

Sometimes we try to squeeze ourselves into situations that don't match who we are, just to fit in or not feel left out—like pretending to like certain things just because everyone else does, or acting a certain way to be accepted. But when you do that, you end up losing parts of yourself. It's like walking around in shoes that are too tight: they hurt, they slow you down, and eventually, you're just uncomfortable all the time.

Knowing what fits you means knowing yourself. It means figuring out what makes you happy, what you believe in, and who you want to be. That takes time—and yeah, sometimes you'll try things that don't work out. But that's part of learning. What matters is that you don't settle for things that don't feel right just because they work for someone else.

It's also a reminder not to compare your life to other people's. Just because a certain path worked for your friend doesn't mean it'll work for you. We all have different goals, dreams, and personalities. And when you stop trying to force what doesn't fit, you make room for what does.

So, if the shoe don't fit, don't wear it. Find your own pair. It might take time, but when it fits, you'll know. And you'll feel way better walking your own path than trying to keep up with someone else's.

FAKE VS REAL FRIENDS – C. DELOATCH

Today we will be talking about fake friends and real friends. First, we're going to talk about choosing your real friends. A real friend will always be there for you no matter what. Real friends will try to stop you from doing dumb stuff. A real friend will be loyal to you. A true friend is someone you can confide in without fear of betrayal.

A fake friend will do this: talk about you to other people, make you date people who you don't want to date, and go around talking about you. A fake friend is someone who pretends to care about you but doesn't genuinely have your best interests at heart—often acting like a friend only when it benefits them, or when they try to manipulate you. Choose your friends wisely.

A little quote: If you're trying to stay out of drama, stop hanging around the ones that stay in drama.

WALKING IN WISDOM – K. PARKER

I have had the privilege of being a member of "Ladies of Distinction" for about four months; however, in the few meetings I've attended, I've learned many ways and methods to become a more distinctive lady.

These ways include:

- Being Yourself
- Saying No
- Conflict Resolution

LIBEROSIS

It's often said that "comparison is the thief of joy." When gathered around so many other great influences, we tend to forget how we are also one of those great influences. In a world that's constantly changing and trying to mold us into what's "trending" or what society accepts as appealing, you have to remember to be you. From an early age, we're told how to talk, how to dress, what is too much or what is too little, but as time goes by, you grow your own opinions and have your own perspectives on things. Being yourself is owning your story, accepting your flaws, and being true to others and yourself. Pretending to fit into the crowd might win approval, but it doesn't bring peace nor true happiness within oneself. Once you realize that just being yourself is enough, you won't yearn for others to accept you anymore, because you've already accepted yourself. And with that being said, always remember, to follow your passions, be weird, be quiet, be loud—and BE YOU.

The world we live in often confuses kindness for weakness. We are taught to say yes and no from a young age, but throughout our lives we constantly fall into the narrative of just being a "yes man," forgetting that it is okay to say no. Most times we do this because we do not want to disappoint others or maybe we're just trying to be polite. But we have to remember: saying no isn't selfish or rude. It's also not just a rejection of others—it's self-awareness and self-respect.

"No" is a complete sentence. It doesn't need an explanation or reason, because you're protecting your time, energy, and peace. You're never obligated to say yes just because someone asks. Saying no creates space and teaches others—and yourself—to value your time and energy. So, the next time you don't want to do something but feel pressured, just remember: you can say no!

No matter where you go, negativity will find a way to try to get to you. Negativity takes many different forms like criticism, toxic environments, failure, self-doubt, etc. The point is—you can't just avoid negativity entirely, because it plays a part in your character development, mental health, growth, and success. Sometimes you'll have people who come into your life and project their insecurities and fears onto you—or just being on social media too much creates a way for comparison and judgment, even of yourself. Most times, the mind is your biggest enemy, constantly fixated on what's next or why something is a certain way.

An effective way of dealing with negativity is learning how to respond. Once you stop giving people the reaction they want, you'll notice how they start to not even bother with you. You have to set boundaries, limit your time with certain people, say no, ignore influences, etc. Navigating negativity is a lifelong journey that requires patience, willingness, and compassion. While we can't always change our circumstances, we can change our mind and perspective to become a stronger version of ourselves—not only being able to brush off negativity but to also rise above it.

CHAPTER 3

LEVELING UP

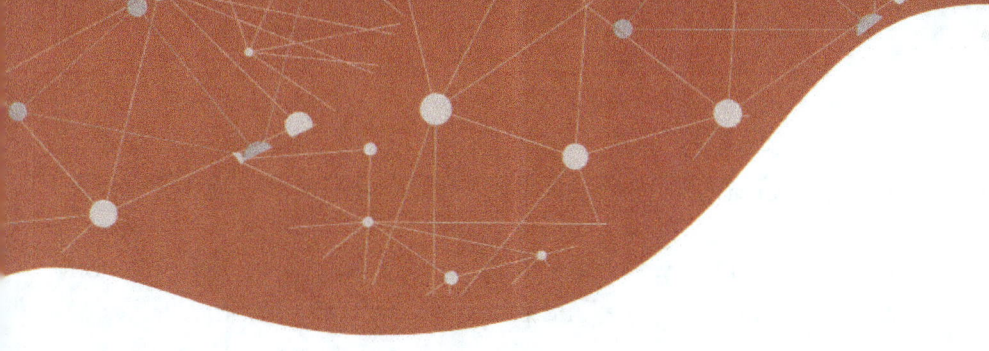

NEVER GIVE UP – S. HARRIS

Never give up on your dream and focus on what matters to you. Stop trying to prove yourself to others. Keep your dreams alive—don't change them for other people. No matter how hard you try, don't let anyone break your heart, and don't give your heart away too fast either. Keep yourself happy. Be around people that actually keep you happy. Never settle for less and help others even if you don't want to. No matter what, help out, because what goes around comes around. Guard your heart—keep it away from people that don't know how to use it and take care of your heart. Never change yourself to fit in and separate yourself from drama by keeping your distance from people that lie on others and use others to get what they want. That's the type of people that you shouldn't hang around with no matter what's said.

EMBRACING WOMEN THROUGH EDUCATION – Z. JOYNER

Throughout history, women have emerged as a powerful motivation for change, resilience, grace, and purpose. Among them, the "ladies of distinction" stand apart, not only through status or praise, but through character, wisdom, and the ability to inspire. Central to their influence is a transformative force: education. It is through education that women are truly embraced, equipped not only to navigate the world but to shape it.

Education is the importance of empowerment. It enables women to think critically, to speak boldly, and to act with intention. A lady of distinction is not defined by circumstance, but by her capacity to lead, to uplift others, and to pursue truth with courage. When a woman is educated, she is given the tools to chart her own course, to rise above limitations, and to illuminate paths for those who follow.

The impact of educated women ripples far beyond the individual. Families flourish, communities grow stronger, and generations benefit from the seeds of knowledge sown in a single life. An educated woman becomes a champion, a caregiver, a visionary, a force for good in every space she inhabits.

To embrace women through education is to invest in the future of society itself. It is to declare that EVERY woman, regardless of background, holds within her the potential to lead with integrity and wisdom. Ladies of distinction are not born; they are educated through opportunity, guidance, and belief in their worth.

Let us, then, be committed to this cause not as a matter of charity, but of justice. In championing the education of women, we do not simply build scholars—we raise nations.

PRACTICING SELF LOVE – A. ROACH

In Ladies of Distinction, you learn it's okay to say no, to be a nice person, and to care for others. One thing that I have learned in L.O.D. is to treat others how you would want to be treated. Being mean to people is not nice. Don't be mean to anybody, because you don't know what they are going through at home. You should always be yourself. Don't let anyone change who you are. If you feel the need to stop being friends with someone because they are trying to change you, then stop being their friend, because if they don't like who you are, then that's not a real friend. Another thing that I have learned in L.O.D. is to guard my heart. That means don't give your love away so fast and be careful who you give your love to. If a boy comes up to you and says, "hey" and gives you a hug, that does not mean that he likes you. Don't let people play around with your feelings. Love yourself, because if you don't put yourself first, you will start to dislike and put yourself down.

More ways to love yourself is to practice self-compassion and engage in self-care. Also, don't let people put you down.

STEPS ON HOW To LOVE YOURSELF:

| STEP 1.

Be kind to yourself.

| STEP 2.

Treat yourself with the same kindness and understanding you would a close friend.

STEP 3.

Forgive yourself. Acknowledge that everyone makes mistakes and learn from them rather than dwelling on them.

STEP 4.

Look after your physical and emotional needs by eating nourishing foods, staying active, and keeping good self-hygiene. This will help how you take care of yourself and feel good about yourself. Some people may ask, what is self-love? Self-love is an appreciation of yourself for who you are. It means showing yourself the same kindness and respect as you would show to anyone else who you love. Another person might ask, why is self-love important? We need self-love in order to get motivated and take on new challenges. It is empowering, and it has a positive impact on stress and on others. Each day, think of something loving you can do for yourself. This could be as simple as a 10-minute break with a book or buying yourself a beautiful bunch of flowers.

TIPS ON HOW TO LOVE YOURSELF:

1. Forgive yourself and let go of shame.

2. Practice self-acceptance and gratitude.

3. Take care of your physical and mental health.

4. Avoid comparing yourself to others.

5. Recognize and validate your feelings.

6. Avoid perfection.

7. Know that it's okay to say no.

Saying no is a fundamental aspect of setting boundaries, respecting your time and energy, and prioritizing your well-being. It allows you to say yes to what truly matters. It also helps you avoid situations that may make you feel uncomfortable or have a bad attitude.

CHAPTER 4

MAX POTENTIAL
SHORT STORIES

THE MIDNIGHT CROSSING: INTO THE REALM OF SHADOWS – L. ASHBURN

THE WHISPERING HOUR

Elias Vale has always been a restless sleeper, but the night he wakes up in Nox is different. At school, he falls asleep during a lecture and wakes up to a world he doesn't recognize. The once-familiar classroom is gone, replaced by an empty field of grey grass stretching out beneath a starless, black sky. His heart races. He's alone, but he can sense something lurking. That's when he hears it—a low whisper that seems to come from all directions.

"You shouldn't be here yet..."

Frozen in place, Elias realizes the whisper isn't coming from a person. It's from something **other**—an entity that feels ancient and malevolent. Shadows shift in the distance, taking form, and for a brief moment, Elias can make out the shape of something monstrous—**The Hollow**.

The Midnight Crossing: Into the Realm of Shadows

It is tall, impossibly thin, its features obscured by the void of night. It watches him but doesn't move.

Elias runs. Just as the creature lunges toward him, he wakes up back in his classroom, breathless and drenched in sweat. The school bell rings. Everything feels... off, but he can't explain why.

SLEEPLESS

Back in the real world, Elias tries to shake the feeling that something's watching him. But the pull of sleep becomes stronger each night. He becomes obsessed with staying awake, avoiding any quiet space where he might drift off. Dark circles form under his eyes, and his body grows weaker by the day.At night, as he lies in bed, he can hear the faintest whisper—like a distant echo of the voice from Nox. He wonders if he's losing his mind. But the nightmares keep coming.

He begins seeing shadowy figures around town—people with dark, hollow eyes that stare at him for just a second before disappearing. Elias's mind starts to unravel. Is he the only one hearing the whispers? Is he the only one who has been to Nox?

THE GIRL IN THE ALLEY

One evening, Elias stumbles across a girl sitting alone in a dark alley. Her name is **Lena**, and she seems to know exactly what he's been experiencing. Lena reveals that she has been to Nox too, and unlike Elias, she's managed to survive multiple trips. But survival comes with a price—she's lost parts of herself in the process, each trip leaving her weaker. Lena has a jagged scar running across her left eye, a remnant of a near-death encounter with the Hollow.

Lena takes Elias to a nearby abandoned building where others like them gather—a small group of survivors who all share the same terrifying experience. They exchange stories of Nox: how some have never woken up, how the Hollow hunts those who wander too far from the waking world. They explain that Nox is a place of broken dreams, where your fears and regrets manifest as twisted creatures.

Elias can't help but ask the question that's been haunting him: *Why is he being pulled into Nox?*

Lena doesn't have the answer, but she warns him that soon he won't be able to tell the difference between waking life and the dream world. When that happens, Nox will consume him completely.

RULES OF THE DREAMWORLD

Lena and the other survivors take Elias deeper into the refuge of their hidden sanctuary, where they discuss the rules of the dreamworld. Time in Nox flows differently from the real world. Sometimes, a single moment can stretch for hours, and sometimes entire days pass in the blink of an eye. Emotions, they explain, are the key to the Hollow's power. Fear, sadness, anger—they act as beacons that attract the monster to those trapped in Nox.

They also reveal a shocking truth: if you die in Nox, you die in real life too. The Hollow feeds on souls, and the longer you're trapped, the more your own soul begins to wither, leaving you vulnerable to its grasp.

Elias learns that the survivors who have managed to escape Nox haven't truly *escaped*—they've just found ways to stave off the Hollow's pull for a time. But every time they sleep, they risk being dragged back.

As Elias tries to process this information, he begins to realize that the Hollow isn't just a random monster—it's hunting **him** specifically. Lena tells him he's not the first to have attracted its attention, and he won't be the last.

ECHOES OF THE PAST

Elias becomes obsessed with finding answers about Nox and the Hollow. He begins to research sleep disorders, lucid dreaming, and old occult practices. In the library at his school, he discovers an old journal written by a former patient of a sleep clinic that was shut down decades ago. The journal details strange dreams, sleep paralysis, and the patient's growing fear that they were being followed by a shadowy figure—much like the Hollow.

The journal's entries stop abruptly after the patient describes a nightmarish event where the creature followed them into their waking world. Elias's pulse quickens as he reads the final entry: *"The Hollow is real, and it comes for those who trespass in its domain."*

Could the sleep clinic be the key to understanding Nox? Elias realizes that the clinic's research into dream states could hold the answer he's looking for. But the more he digs, the more questions arise, and the closer he gets to the truth, the more dangerous things become.

SLEEP TRIALS

Desperate for answers, Elias agrees to undergo a sleep study at a nearby clinic. It's his only chance to understand why he's being pulled into Nox and what the Hollow really wants. The clinic uses experimental technology to monitor his brain activity during sleep, and Elias hopes they'll uncover something about the connection between Nox and his dreams.

As the procedure begins, Elias falls into a deep sleep. But instead of just entering Nox like before, he finds himself trapped in a **nightmare version of the clinic**. The walls are twisted, the hallways are endless, and the machines beep erratically. The Hollow, now a distorted, more monstrous version of itself, hunts him through the corridors. Elias can feel its presence, its cold, empty eyes watching him.

Just as the creature lunges, Elias wakes up with a start. The scientists at the clinic are confused—his brainwaves showed no signs of disturbance during the study. But when Elias looks at his arm, he notices something strange: **a scar**—the same scar that Lena has. A physical mark from Nox. His body has begun to carry the marks of his dreams.

THE HOLLOW AWAKENS

The Hollow is no longer confined to the dream world. Elias begins to see glimpses of it in his waking life—its shadow lurking just outside his peripheral vision, its haunting presence closing in. One night, as he walks home, Elias sees a familiar face—the face of **Lena**, but something is wrong. She's not just a girl anymore; she's a **hollowed shell**, her eyes empty and lifeless.

Before he can react, she vanishes into the shadows. Elias's fear intensifies—he knows the Hollow is closing in on him. As the boundary between dreams and reality blurs, he struggles to hold on to his sense of self. If the Hollow gets too close, it will claim his soul just like it claimed Lena's.

THE CITY BENEATH SLEEP

Elias returns to Nox, determined to find a way out. He stumbles upon a hidden city—**The City Beneath Sleep**—a place where the forgotten dreams of many people have taken root. It's a place of fractured memories and lost hopes. Here, survivors of the Hollow's hunt have built a refuge, hiding from the creature and fighting to stay alive.

The city is ruled by an enigmatic figure—**Elder Ios**, a dreamer who has spent centuries trapped in Nox. Ios reveals that Nox is not just a place of nightmares; it's a prison, built by an ancient force that manipulates the very fabric of dreams. To escape, Elias must uncover the truth about Nox's creation and confront the entity that controls it—the **Dreamweaver**.

THE DREAMER'S KEY

In the heart of the city, Elias uncovers an old library filled with forbidden texts. He finds a prophecy written long ago by dreamers who foresaw the coming of **The Dreamer**—someone who would have the power to either destroy or free Nox. But the prophecy is vague, and Elias doesn't fully understand what it means.

The only way to learn more is to venture deeper into Nox, past the Hollow's domain, and find the Dreamweaver's lair. But Elias isn't alone. The Hollow has sensed his presence and is growing more dangerous. Time is running out.

THE DREAMWEAVER'S LAIR

Elias, now determined to confront the Dreamweaver, prepares to journey deeper into Nox, where the rules of reality bend and break. He knows the Hollow is following him, growing stronger with each passing night, and if he doesn't act soon, he'll lose himself entirely.

Lena's fate weighs heavily on him. She was one of the first to warn him about Nox, and now, her absence feels like a shadow following his every step. Elias is afraid that he, too, will become just another lost soul in this twisted dreamscape.

As Elias ventures deeper into the heart of Nox, the landscape changes. The once-empty fields give way to towering, jagged mountains made of shattered glass and twisted metal. His senses are assaulted by disorienting sights and sounds. At the summit, a massive fortress looms ahead—the **Dreamweaver's Lair**.

Inside, Elias faces not just the Dreamweaver, but a **manifestation of his own fears**: a distorted version of himself, taunting him with every self-doubt he's ever had. In the Dreamweaver's Lair, Elias learns the horrifying truth about his connection to Nox—the Hollow isn't just hunting him. It's been drawn to him because he is the **key** to Nox's creation. Elias's ability to travel between worlds, to slip between reality and the dream, has made him a **living anchor** to this realm. The Hollow is his reflection, his twisted counterpart in the dream world. And now, Elias must make a choice: embrace his connection to Nox and become a vessel for the Hollow, or break free and destroy the dream realm.

BREAKING THE DREAM

Elias stands at the precipice of everything—his destiny, his fears, and the fate of both Nox and the waking world. In the Dreamweaver's lair, he's forced to confront the **true origin of Nox**: it was created from the **collective dreams** of humanity, a place where their fears and hopes collide. But the realm has become corrupted over time, manipulated by those who entered it—including Elias's own father, a famous scientist who once sought to use dream technology for human advancement, but disappeared without a trace years ago.

Elias realizes that Nox was never meant to be a prison. It was a place for **exploration**, a realm where people could confront their darkest fears in a controlled environment. But the interference of power-hungry minds corrupted the dreamscape, twisting it into a hunting ground for the Hollow and those like it.

The choice is agonizing. If Elias destroys the Dreamweaver, Nox could collapse, trapping everyone within it forever. But if he embraces his connection to Nox, he could become a part of the dreamworld, feeding the Hollow and allowing it to grow even stronger.

THE RISE OF THE CONFIDENCE CRUSADER – T. GAY

THE STORMY NIGHT

Jay is introduced as an ordinary 13-year-old boy in middle school. We learn about his struggles with bullying and feeling invisible among his peers. One stormy night, while working on a science project, lightning strikes him, causing a life-changing event.

AWAKENING OF POWER

After waking up from a ten-day coma, Jay discovers he has gained incredible superpower confidence. He feels different but doesn't fully understand why. As he returns to school, he faces his bullies for the first time, standing up for himself and surprising everyone around him.

THE SCIENCE PRESENTATION

In class, it's time for presentations. Jay's two greatest enemies are ready to undermine him, filling him with fear and doubt. However, he remembers his new power and pushes through, delivering an impressive presentation that earns him applause from classmates and teachers alike.

A HERO EMERGES

Later that day, Jay witnesses an old lady being robbed. Fueled by his newfound courage, he rushes to help her, confronting the thief and retrieving her purse. This act of heroism solidifies his identity as "The Confidence Crusader," inspiring him to embrace his role as a protector.

EMBRACING HIS DESTiNY

As Jay continues to navigate middle school life, he learns how to balance his powers with everyday challenges. He begins to inspire other students to stand up against bullying and support one another. In this chapter, we see jay grow into his superhero persona, making a positive impact on his school community.

FIRST RESCUE

Jay, now embracing his role as The Confidence Crusader, starts patrolling his neighborhood after school. He notices a fire in an apartment building. People are trapped on the upper floors. Using his confidence, he directs the crowd and helps calm the panicked residents. He finds a way to get inside and guides the trapped residents to safety, using his quick thinking and newfound courage.

THE DOUBTERS

Jay's double life starts to take a toll. He's tired, and his grades begin to slip. Some classmates become suspicious of his frequent disappearances and sudden bursts of confidence. A rival student, jealous of Jay's newfound popularity, tries to expose him as a fraud. Jay must learn to balance his responsibilities as a student and a hero while dealing with the challenges of maintaining his secret identity.

THE BULLY'S BROTHER

Jay discovers that the older brother of one of his former bullies is involved in petty crimes around the neighborhood. He confronts the brother, hoping to deter him from his criminal activities. The situation escalates, leading to a physical confrontation where Jay must use his powers responsibly, avoiding serious harm. Jay realizes that being a hero isn't just about physical strength but also about making difficult choices and understanding the consequences of his actions.

THE CONFIDENCE CRISIS

Jay faces a situation where his confidence is shaken. He tries to save someone, but his efforts fail, leading to a negative outcome. He begins to doubt his abilities and questions whether he's truly cut out to be a hero. He confides in a trusted adult—perhaps a teacher or family member, who helps him understand that even heroes make mistakes and that true strength lies in learning from them.

A HERO'S RESOLVE

Jay regains his confidence by focusing on the positive impact he's made and the people he's helped. He realizes that his power isn't just about physical abilities but also about inspiring others to believe in themselves. He returns to his role as The Confidence Crusader with renewed determination, ready to face whatever challenges lie ahead.

UNMASKED

During a rescue, Jay's mask is accidentally knocked off, and his face is caught on a news camera. The footage goes viral, and Jay's identity as The Confidence Crusader is revealed to the world. His classmates, teachers, and neighbors are shocked to learn that the quiet, unassuming Jay is the hero they've been reading about.

PARENTAL CONCERNS

Jay's parents are terrified when they discover his secret. They worry about his safety and the risks he's taking. They ground him and forbid him from using his powers, fearing that he'll get seriously hurt or worse. Jay is torn between his desire to help people and his responsibility to obey his parents.

THE DEBATE

Jay tries to explain to his parents why he feels compelled to use his powers for good. He argues that he's making a positive difference in the community and that he's careful and responsible. His parents remain unconvinced, emphasizing the dangers and the potential consequences of his actions. The chapter explores the conflict between Jay's personal calling and his parents' protective instincts.

DEFIANCE

Despite his parents' ban, Jay can't ignore the calls for help. He feels a responsibility to use his powers for good. He starts sneaking out at night, continuing his hero work in secret, careful to avoid detection. The guilt of disobeying his parents weighs on him, but he justifies his actions by telling himself that he's helping people who need it.

A CHANGE OF HEART

Jay's parents eventually discover that he's been defying them. They are initially furious and feel betrayed. However, after seeing a news report of Jay saving a group of people from a dangerous situation, they begin to understand his passion and dedication. They realize that they can't stop him from being a hero, but they can help him do it safely and responsibly. They make a deal with Jay: he can continue being The Confidence Crusader, but only if he maintains good grades and keeps them informed of his activities. Jay agrees, grateful for their understanding and support. He promises to balance his responsibilities as a student and a hero, knowing that he has the love and trust of his family behind him.

A NEW ALLY

Jay meets a new student at school who has recently moved to the neighborhood. This student is curious about Jay's superhero activities and offers to help him with his missions. Jay is hesitant to involve others in his hero's work due to safety concerns but realizes that having an ally could be beneficial. They team up for a small mission, learning to trust each other and combining their strengths.

THE RIVAL'S CHALLENGE

The rival student from earlier challenges Jay to a public debate or competition, questioning his motives and abilities as a hero. Jay must prepare to defend his actions and prove that his intentions are genuine. Through the debate, Jay demonstrates his confidence and sincerity, earning respect from peers and even softening the rival's stance.

COMMUNITY CRISIS

Jay seeks advice from a trusted teacher or mentor who has noticed his struggles balancing school and hero duties. The mentor challenges Jay to think about long-term goals and the impact he wants to have beyond immediate heroics. Jay gains valuable insights into leadership and responsibility, helping him refine his approach to being a hero.

THE VILLAIN'S RETURN

The older brother of the bully returns, now involved in more serious criminal activities. He targets Jay, seeking revenge for past confrontations. Jay faces a direct threat to his safety and must strategize to protect himself and those around him. Using his confidence and quick thinking, Jay outmaneuvers the villain, leading to his capture and reinforcing Jay's role as a protector.

A HERO'S LEGACY

As the school year ends, Jay reflects on his journey and the changes he's seen in himself and his community. He considers what it means to leave a lasting legacy and how he can continue inspiring others. Jay decides to start a club or initiative focused on empowerment and anti-bullying, ensuring his impact continues even when he's not actively patrolling.

MISUNDERSTOOD – R. KAIWAN

Jim sees his friend Zack playing with the other team and "trash talking" him.Zack - "Jim, wait. I thought maybe you wanted me to play on their team It's just—I can't take it when I'm on your team. You always complain about every mistake, so I wanted to play against you and tell you about your weak points, because you wanted to be a famous soccer player. I wanted to make you the best of the best with my heads-up. So let's do another match, but me and you together against some randoms."

Jim - "Heh, bet. Let's do this". They both look at each other and join the soccer match. Both of them using every moment with the ball to shine brighter and brighter. They perform great and difficult skills, and the other team loses by 2 points.

Random person - "Hey, you two are amazing at soccer! You should try signing up for some leagues—they will definitely take you, trust."

Zack - "Hey let's do it."

Jim - "I mean, we have to it's the easiest way to become famous." So they sign up, and with time they become known as the Deadly Defender-Shooter Duo—so lethal that no one underestimates them.

Zack - "Hey, we're famous now! What's our next goal? To have our own brands?"

Jim - "Nah, be more egotistical with me. I want us to get the World Cup."

Zack - "Alright then, let's practice harder than ever."

After a few years, they win the World Cup and become inspiration to others.

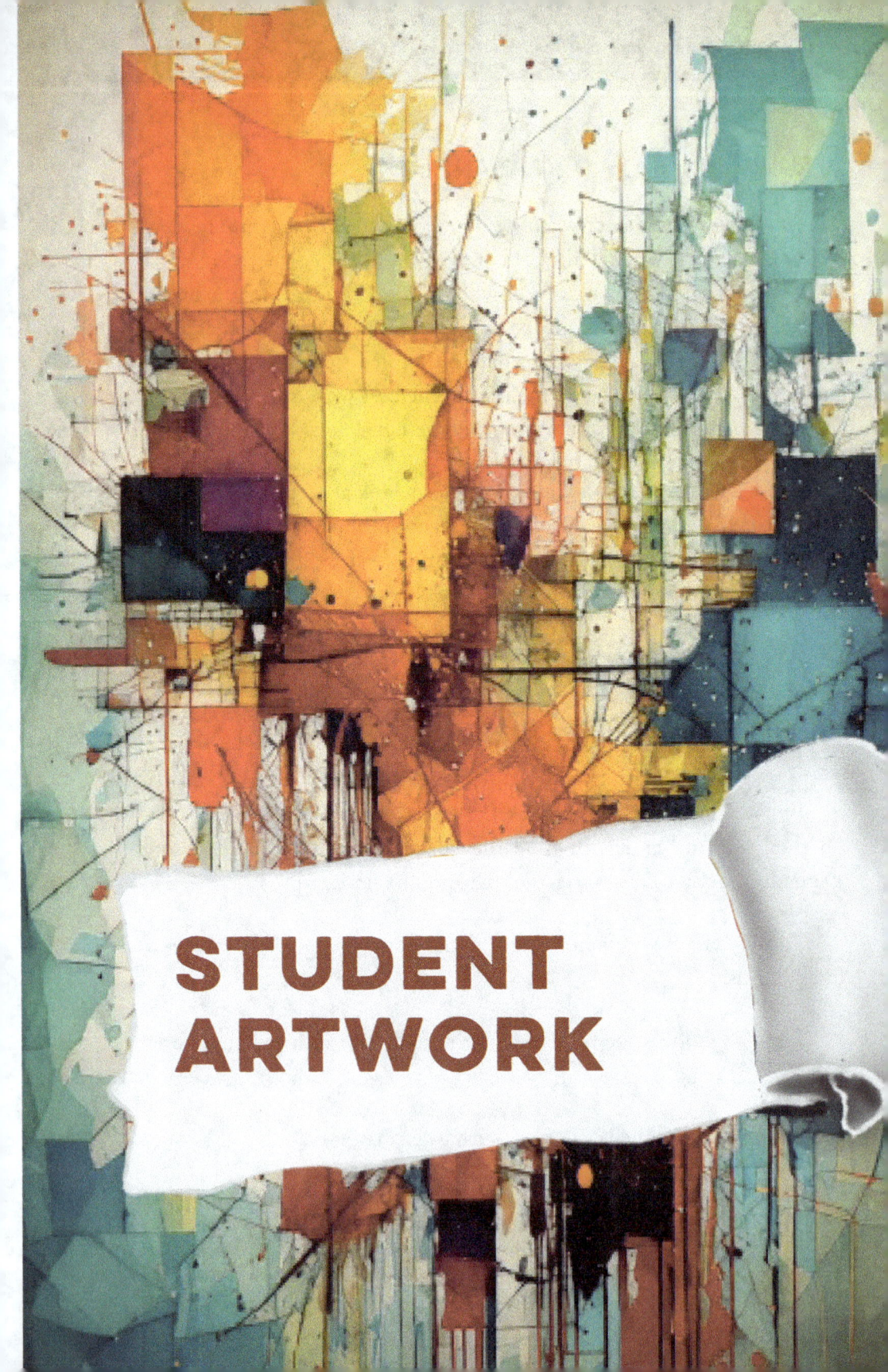

STUDENT
ARTWORK

www.ingramcontent.com/pod-product-compliance
Lightning Source LLC
Chambersburg PA
CBHW071352130626
46556CB00005B/2142

9 798991 562225